I0794776

POLAR BABIES

SNOWY OWLETS

by Genevieve Nilsen

TABLE OF CONTENTS

Words to Know 2

Snowy Owlets 3

Let's Review! 16

Index 16

tadpole books

WORDS TO KNOW

feathers

feet

fly

nest

owlets

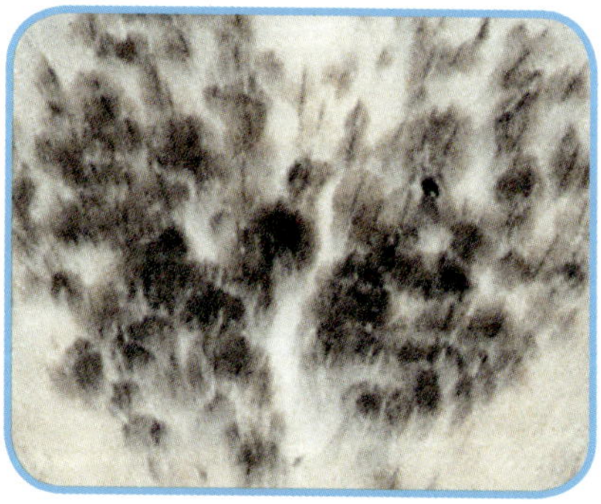

spots

SNOWY OWLETS

Look! Snowy owlets!

They are gray.

They are in a nest.

Mom and dad are white.

Dad brings food.

spot

Mom has spots.

They grow.

They turn white.

Feathers keep them warm.

Even on their feet!

They fly!

LET'S REVIEW!

An owlet has feathers and feet. It has a beak and wings, too. Can you point to them?

INDEX

dad 6, 7

feathers 12

feet 13

fly 15

mom 6, 9

nest 5

owlets 3

spots 9